The

MAGIC

of Symbolism

Enrich Your Writing
With
Hidden Meaning

Autumn Bardot

The Magic of Symbolism
Enrich Your Writing with Hidden Meaning

Flores Publishing

Cover design: Sweet & Spicy Designs

Interior formatting: Sweet & Spicy Designs

ISBN paperback: 978-1-7340897-4-5

DISCLAIMER

Any views or opinions represented in are personal and belong solely to the owner and do not represent those of people, institutions, or organizations that the owner may or may not be associated with in a professional or personal capacity, unless explicitly stated. Any views or opinions are not intended to malign any religion, ethnic group, club, organization, company, or individual.

All content provided is for informational purposes only. The author makes no representation as to the accuracy or completeness of any information or references to source material. The author will not be liable for any errors or omission in this information nor for the availability of this information.

THE MAGIC OF SYMBOLISM

ENRICH YOUR WRITING WITH HIDDEN MEANING

AUTUMN BARDOT

CONTENTS

1. Write a More Powerful Story   1
2. How To Use This Information   6
3. Setting   8
4. Direction   11
5. Hot & Cold   13
6. Religion   17
7. Shapes   20
8. Architecture   25
9. Blood   32
10. Body   36
11. Eyes   45
12. Color   50
13. Color Descriptors   56
14. What Nots   59
15. Clothing   67
16. Fire & Water   69
17. More Water   73
18. Illness   75
19. Light & Dark   78
20. Sex   81
21. Mealtime   85
22. Topography   89
23. Weather   93
24. Violence   97
25. Nature   100
26. Seasons   108
27. Animals & Critters   112
28. Final Thoughts   119

About the Author   121
Other Books by Autumn Bardot   123

ONE

WRITE A MORE POWERFUL STORY

Reading has always been my passion. I was the nerdy girl in high school who preferred novels to parties. Always had a book with me. Occasionally penned silly stories for my friends. Was the family's eulogy writer. Reading seemed infinitely more interesting than anything happening in my corner of the world.

Reading is true freedom. It allows me to travel to places and times, be a thousand people, and have a host of experiences. You know, the usual. I was a voracious reader, reading novels far beyond my understanding and lexicon level.

I became a language arts teacher. It was a natural extension of that biblio-passion. I had always wanted to write a book—even wrote a pretty horrible story when I was twelve—but didn't feel I had anything interesting to write about. Mind you, this was before the internet—I've just dated myself —and the easy access of a world of information. But then a marvelous thing happened. No, not the internet.

I began to teach in an advanced, high-stakes language arts program. I *thought* I knew my stuff. I had a degree in English Literature, after all. I was wrong. The exams required students to analyze literature in great depth. Determined not to let the students down and embarrass myself, I read books about literary analysis and rhetoric. What happened was marvelous. I discovered how a few choice words can have a profound impact on character, conflict, plot, foreshadowing, emotion, and theme.

I remember the day I decided to try my hand at writing a novel. I graduated with my Masters in Curriculum and Instruction and had the summer off. Finally! A chance to do what I wanted: Write a novel!!

I attended conferences, wrote, and rewrote ad nauseum. I learned a lot about the elements of storytelling, but one thing I noticed was the lack of workshops about the **power of words**, about how word choice is often imbued with **symbolic meaning, nuance, subtext, connotation, and feelings** found deep within our collective consciousness.

Many aspiring writers describe characters or events without understanding or wielding their god-like power to amplify characterization, conflict, or emotion.

Use your word power!

Don't believe in the power of words? Take a quick look at any social media platform and see how the wrong word will have the social media mob *crucify* the hapless commenter. See what I did there? I used the word *crucify* and you were okay with it. You understood the connotative definition. But what if I used the word *lynched?* Would you cringe, be annoyed or upset? I wouldn't be surprised. *Lynched* is a loaded word, one linked to a horrific time in US history. And yet *crucify* is equally horrific. Both are cruel ways to die.

Any traditionally published author will tell you of a time when their editor suggested a change because a particular word was a trigger word, the unintended offending word provoking gut-deep offensive feelings and emotions in a reader. In the writer's case, that word is bad magic because it does not produce the tone or mood we want to convey. The reader gets turned off. Not good.

I often review students' college essays and personal statements. I point out the words and phrases—that they wrote—that make them seem arrogant, rude, silly, ignorant, immature, or ungrateful. Usually, all it takes is a few word tweaks and, presto, they sound like the perfect candidate for college.

But this little book is not about trigger and politically correct words. It's about using the power of words and symbols to enhance our story in the right magical way!

An English literature degree and teaching literary analysis makes me appreciate and understand how to write a more impactful sentence. It helps me to be mindful of words and symbols and allows me to play with them to evoke emotion.

Words are magic. Symbols are powerful magic

If an author writes, "the blood-red velvet drapes concealed the dirt-encrusted window" the words *blood, velvet, concealed,* and *dirt-encrusted* convey more than just random descriptive detail. *Blood* has a myriad of connotations. *Velvet* suggests luxury, and/or wealth. The word *conceal* implies something altogether different than if the word *covered* was used. *Dirt-encrusted* may imply multiple meanings; slovenliness, or how the author or characters view the world. The short description is a clue, one providing thematic, foreshadowing, context, plot, and characterization beyond the superficial.

This is a quick guide, a springboard meant for

you to leap high and dive into powerful word choices

Does this mean you *have* to write like that? No, of course not! It is only another way to add depth, nuance, and complexity. Study your genre. Learn what works best and what the reader expects. Let the word magic come forth organically from the plot and characters. Conjure up the best word choice during revisions.

Context is important. And irony trumps everything! That's right! The sun can shine, the birds sing, the path be wide and even, and the character can be doomed!

WARNING!

Including symbolic language in an effort to sound literary adds nothing to your story. But when the story warrants it, the writer can open up their symbolism toolbox to add depth, nuance, and context to enrich characters, scenes, foreshadowing, plot, and emotions.

TWO

HOW TO USE THIS INFORMATION

There's a lot of information here. Too much to digest in one sitting. Too much to remember. Give it a quick look over and then use this little book as a resource while you write.

Look for the CONSIDERATIONS section for each topic and subtopic for questions to ask yourself about how and why you may want to integrate and enrich your character and stories. It's easy to find. CONSIDERATIONS has a different font and is identified by arrows.

Let's say you're writing a scene about two would-be lovers walking somewhere. Do you want to foreshadow or provide additional characterization? You can! Do they walk in a garden, park, forest, or on a cracked city sidewalk? Does one of them trip? Or both? Are they wearing clothes that indicate their personality? Is the female wearing business attire but a fun kitschy bracelet? Is the male wearing a staid suit and tie with Hawaiian print socks? What color are their outfits? Are they going uphill or downhill? Is the path curved or straight? Check out the chapter on clothing, color symbolism, and topography.

All these can add clues to a character's personality, conflict, and emotion. Is it a bright sunny day? Cold and windy? Even the weather, if you choose, can foreshadow their relationship. Why do you think Shakespeare's stage direction often included thunder and lightning before a particularly ominous scene?

THREE

SETTING

Setting is more than just location.

Usually when folks think of setting in the literary sense, they think of a physical location. But setting is much more than that. Authors construct setting like they do characters and plot.

Setting is a powerful element for establishing themes and often reflect the author's own background, biases, and perspectives. Setting can influence, shape, and emphasize a character's actions and ideas. It can drive plot, create mood, or assume the role of antagonist.

Settings can be:

- Political
- Time specific (minutes, hours, days, months, years, decades)

- Historical
- Financial
- Socio-economic
- Cultural
- Religious
- Dystopian/utopian
- Geographical
- Regional
- Magical
- Mythical
- Surreal
- Constructed/ alternate /parallel/imaginary
- Dream (think *Inception*)
- Virtual (think *Tron)*
- Psychological
- Attitudinal
- Industrial
- Seasonal
- A specific, physical place
- Temperature
- Climate
- Weather
- Geography
- Landscape/topography

CONSIDERATIONS

▸ What role does your setting play in your story?

▸ How important/to what degree?

▸ What setting will let your story and characters shine?

FOUR

DIRECTION

Direction can be tricky depending on if you are from the eastern or western hemisphere. Europe and North American authors have assigned literary symbolism to the four directions. You'll see why in a moment.

North is traditionally associated with colder weather. It is linked to austerity, starkness, industriousness, isolation, cold-heartedness, hostility, and bitterness. Like the thick layers necessary to protect one from the cold (be it psychological, spiritual, or emotional) a character wears these layers as protection.

South is warm temperatures and sunny climes. It's where the wealthy went for rest and relaxation. It is associated with plenty, hedonism, clothing removal, and the hot sweaty acts one engages in when naked. It is where a character's lusts, passions, and subconscious motives are exposed.

West: The symbolism of this direction might be an American thing. Freedom from rules, freedom from laws, adventure, fresh starts, and possibilities are associated with this direction. In Mark Twain's *Huck Finn*, Huck and Jim decide to (spoiler alert) go west where they will be free from the racism and prejudices they encounter in their journey on the Mississippi River. Ayn Rand's Atlas *Shrugged* is another example. John Galt and his groupies hide out in a valley in the west.

East: Exotic and mysterious, it is linked to renewal, rebirth, early civilizations, and the location of the Garden of Eden. (Kind of vague directions if you ask me.) It's also associated with wealth and corruption.

Not convinced? Think of the geography of *Game of Thrones*. It is a fictional world and George R.R. Martin could have set the saga in the southern hemisphere, but he didn't. Even the name Stark is descriptive of a cold northern landscape.

Before your characters head off somewhere, you might want to consider if direction is important.

FIVE

HOT & COLD

Temperature symbolism is hot hot hot. Turn it up for burning anger or passion that sizzles. Turn it down to reveal character and mood. But be careful, the heated adjectives can be ambiguous in the cold reality of writing.

Temperature can:

- Reveal a novel's overall mood
- Be a plot device
- Reveal a character's personality
- Reveal a character's mood
- Be thematic

The Great Gatsby is loaded with heat. Tom is a hot-head. Gatsby is hot for Daisy. Tom is hot (lusting) for Myrtle and hot (with anger) when he discovers Daisy's infidelity. Myrtle is hot to be wealthy. Gatsby made all his money on hot goods. Myrtle's husband is hot to murder his wife's killer. The rising temperature mirrors the rising anger/lust of the characters.

Heat, and all its scorching synonyms, can refer to:

- Lust: He got hot just looking at her.
- Personality: He's a hot head.
- Anger: Tom grew hot when he learned Daisy cheated on him with Gatsby.
- Popularity: Every writer dreams of being the next hot new author.
- Enthusiasm: He was hot for the next new novel by his favorite author.
- Physical attractiveness: Damn, his chiseled body is hot.
- Actual temperature: There are many descriptive words for hot, be sure to choose the one that reveals just *how* hot.

Heated words can refer to:

- Lust
- Love
- Anger
- Embarrassment
- Guilt

- Shame

Synonyms

warm, summery, tropical, broiling, boiling, searing, blistering, sweltering, torrid, sultry, humid, muggy, roasting, baking, scorching, scalding, searing, heated, red-hot, steamy

Cold may refer to:

- Personality: The boss in *The Devil Wears Prada* is cold-hearted.
- Lack of emotion: His response to my question was cold.
- Remoteness: The detectives knew their leads were cold, but they looked for clues anyway.
- Improbability: It will be a cold day in hell when I forgive you.
- Austerity: Some folks think that modern furniture is cold-looking.
- Actual temperature

Chilly words can refer to anger, indifference, death, reality, conviction, cruelty

Synonyms

chilly, chill, cool, freezing, icy, nippy, wintry, frosty, frigid, bitter, biting, raw, bone-chilling, arctic, frozen, numb, shivery

Whether you're writing his *arctic* glare

sent *chills* down my spine or her *smoldering* gaze *lit* my desires on *fire,* have fun lowering or raising the temperature in your stories.

SIX

RELIGION

In the western world, the Judeo-Christian concepts and the bible are engrafted into our collective conscience. Many people, even non-believers, know a bible story or two, which is why writers add depth and complexity with its timeless themes of betrayal, sin, fall from grace, loss of innocence, goodness, evil, and redemption.

A religious symbol, parable, or name can:

- Explain or amplify a theme, scene, or conflict
- Add irony
- Satirize
- Condemn
- Foreshadow
- Characterize a person or place
- Allude to a person, place, or thing

Biblical Heavy Hitters

- Biblical names like Mary, Noah, Eve, Solomon, Jesus, & Joseph
- Idyllic gardens that characters get kicked out or leave
- Biblical numbers like 7 days and 40 days
- One brother killing another
- Serpents – can't get any more of a universal iconic symbol than a snake
- Plagues – it's old school wrath of God stuff
- Floods – one that washes evil away
- Sermons on hills – lectures on grassy knolls work too
- Crown of thorns - In *Dead Poet's Society*, Neil wears Puck's crown before shooting himself.
- No room at the inn – because 'they' never can accommodate the little people
- Crucifixion. One can be crucified on social media too.
- Escape from slavery – lead a whole bunch of others out for more symbolic oomph
- Wandering in a desert – make sure to have some enlightenment, new understanding, or epiphany at the end
- Milk and honey – milk is nutritious,

honey is sweet. Sweet nourishment is a win-win for all!

- Being tempted by Satan. Recall the famous scene from *Lord of the Flies*?
- Carpenter occupation – a hobby works just as well
- Twelve friends, one of which will betray you.
- Last supper

What about other religions?

Read novels and poems from other countries/cultures and expect allusions to Islam, Buddhism, Judaism, Hinduism, Shintoism, etc., and their corresponding holy scriptures and/or beliefs. Remember, if the reader is unfamiliar with the religion, they will not be able to identify the religious allusions or symbolism.

CONSIDERATIONS

▶ Does your character have a biblical name for a reason?

▶ Is the name ironic?

▶ Does the name foreshadow?

▶ Is the name thematic?

▶ What is the purpose of the biblical allusion?

SEVEN

SHAPES

Circles and squares and triangles and stars, oh my! Before man carved pictographs and told the gods' tales in cuneiform, shapes denoted meanings and were imbued with mystical power.

Circles & Spheres

- Universal symbol of completeness and perfection
- God
- Sphere of heaven
- Circle of life
- Movements of the stars and heavens
- Hindus and Buddhists associate it with birth, death, and rebirth
- Wheel of Law in Buddhism
- A round table (Early management style

first practiced by the legendary King
Arthur.)

- Denotes equality, all stakeholders having
  an equal share in solving a problem
- Dante saw Hell as a series of concentric
  circles.
- A ring denotes a pledge or promise.
- A sphere represents the spiritual aspect
  of heaven/universe, which is why domes
  top many religious buildings.

Spiral

- Energy
- Spirals drawn in a woman's womb
  indicate fertility.
- The helix is also a fertility symbol and
  the double helix has become the visual
  representation of DNA. Guess those
  ancients were on to something!

Triangle

- Associated with the number three
- Beginning, middle, and end
- Trinity of gods
- Body, soul, and spirit
- Man, woman, and child

- An upward pointing equilateral triangle represents the male sex part.
- Fire
- A downward pointing triangle is the symbol for a woman or her female parts.
- Water
- The base of a pyramid represents the earth; the apex, heaven.

Squares & Cubes

- A pausing or suspension
- Stability
- Lasting perfection
- The four directions
- In Islam, it represents the heart's susceptibility to the divine, angelic, human, and diabolic forces.
- Square halos in Christian art indicates the person was alive when painted.
- A cube is symbolic of the material universe.
- Wisdom, veracity, and moral fortitude
- The cloistered courtyard of religious structures indicates endurance and security.

Stars

- Wisdom
- Spiritual counsel
- Light of wisdom shining in the dark, sinful world
- Mythological figures or deities
- The dead
- The Star of Bethlehem symbolizes Christ's birth
- A 5-pointed pentagram pointed upwards represents a human (the top point is the head; the sides, arms; the lower points, legs.)
- Flip the pentagram around and it's the sign of the devil—the two upward pointing points are the devil's horns.
- A 6-pointed hexagram—2 interlocking triangles— is symbolic of: 1) the conjoining of male and female; 2) the four elements; 3) Star of David; and 4) Judaism.
- A 7-pointed heptagram is: 1) a magic symbol for pagans; 2) symbolic of the 7 days of creation; and 3) the 7 steps of enlightenment for Buddhists.

Crosses

- Different configurations have different meanings, origins, and significance.

- Christianity
- The shape predates Christianity
- Sacred shape to Ancient Egyptians and Aztecs

Mandala

- Not a shape per se but a pattern
- Search for inner peace or spiritual enlightenment
- Pathway to the Divine or God
- A symbolic trap for malevolent spirits
- Used as a tool or focal point in meditation
- Universe

CONSIDERATIONS

▸ How and why is the shape of an object, home, room, or space in your novel relevant?

EIGHT

ARCHITECTURE

The roof overhead, the window gazed through, the threshold walked across, all these structural features can be used symbolically.

Window

- Allows in the light of knowledge/ understanding.
- Allows character to view the outside world, which may or may not be a good thing.

CONSIDERATIONS

▸ Are the windows dirty or clean?
▸ Are the drapes/ blinds closed or open?
▸ Stained glass, especially those with religious iconography, shout RELIGION, and may

reveal that the character views the world through the dogma of their religion.

▸ Who's looking out the window?

▸ The window itself (big, small, clean, dirty, etched)

▸ How they look out– gaze (longing), peek (fearful), gawk (surprise), or is the character simply avoiding what's going on inside

▸ The view

▸ Who do they see? What they see? City, pastoral, suburbs, mountains, swamps, rain, sunshine?

Door

- Divide between good and evil
- Transition from one stage of life to another
- Divide between one world and another
- Locked doors suggest secrets and forbidden places/worlds/experiences

CONSIDERATIONS

▸ Size of the door. A huge door may make character feel either insignificant or important

▸ Condition of the door

▸ Door style: gothic, modern, medieval, modern

‣ What events or people wait on the other side of the door?

‣ Door to what? A room, attic, home, basement

Archway

- Divine or religious entrance into another state of being
- Rebirth
- Metaphysical time-space threshold

CONSIDERATIONS

‣ What spiritual, attitudinal, religious world does the character experience? Is it external, internal, or both?

Wall

- Strength
- Division or barrier
- Privacy

CONSIDERATIONS

‣ Who is building an emotional wall?

‣ What/who is being kept in?

‣ What/who is being kept out?

Floor

- Earthy realm
- Being grounded in reality
- Flooring type may be symbolic. Is it marble (wealth) or rustic wood (humility)?

CONSIDERATIONS

▸ Is the floor swept clean? Dirty? Dusty? Worn? Polished? Simple? Ornate? Extravagant?

Roof

- Shelter
- Keeps evil out
- Roof shape may be suggestive.
- Domed roofs are emblematic of heaven
- Low roofs suggest restriction or being hemmed in by dogmas.
- Vaulted roofs may be a metaphor for high-mindedness or lofty ideals.

Hallway

- Transitional space

- May mirror the character's transitional emotions, conflicts, quest, or purpose
- Location before deciding which symbolic door the character will enter

Stair/Steps

- Steps towards or away from morality, knowledge, power, or enlightenment
- Winding staircases suggest mystery. One can't see straight ahead.

Kitchen

- Traditional domain of women
- Maternal care taking, be it with food, spiritual, or motherly nourishment
- Best place for your characters to get their hands on a knife
- A character's kitchen reveals their personality.

CONSIDERATIONS

▸ Who's in the kitchen may indicate who is the caretaker.
▸ What's being 'cooked?' Food, a scheme

Living room/Drawing room

- Room where proper social behavior was expected
- Location of one's public persona

CONSIDERATIONS

▸ What's the condition of the room?
▸ Who is being received/ turned away?
▸ Is dirty laundry aired or concealed?
▸ Are there furtive looks?
▸ Are the characters on public display?

Bedroom

- Love
- Lust
- Private room where one's true self appears

CONSIDERATIONS

▸ Is the décor lavish, sparse, childlike?
▸ Does the room reflect the character's personality?

Library

- Synonymous with learning, knowledge, and education

- Place of ancient wisdom or secrets

CONSIDERATIONS

▸ What's being revealed?
▸ What's the condition of the library?
▸ Is the discovery surprising, confusing, enlightening, damning, etc.

Attic

- Storeroom of tucked away memories and secrets
- Place of half-remembered or forgotten truths
- Storage for relics of the family's or ancestor's past

Basement

- Deepest darkest secrets
- Underworld or lower realms
- Creepy or base desires

Which room will you put your characters in? And why?

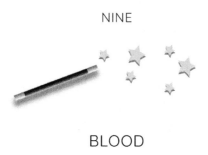

NINE

BLOOD

Blood is a powerful and often confusing symbol. From the divine to the violent, our fascination with blood infuses our collective consciousness. An entire book could be devoted to the symbolism of blood. And perhaps already Is.

The reason behind the power of blood is obvious. Blood is LIFE. A physical indicator of our existence. And yet, behind this crimson liquid life force, man has imbued blood with great spiritual, divine, and emotional dominion.

Bloody Diction

- Bloodline: A line or sequence of ancestors. In some primitive Amazonian tribes, shaman are forbidden to taint their bloodline, for to do so destroys and corrupts their mystical powers.

- Bloodlines produced royal dynasties, perpetuated genetic anomalies and disorders, or got your kinsmen slaughtered.
- Bloodlust: Intense desire to see people killed
- Bloodbath: A fight that ends with death and dismemberment, or a struggle that ends with a group's total destruction.
- Blueblood: A member, usually by bloodline, who comes from old historic aristocracy.
- Oxblood: A really weird name for a color, don't you agree?
- Cold-blooded: Adjective to describe actions done without emotion or concern for others' emotions or consequences.
- Hot-blooded: Adjective describing one whose actions are determined by intense emotions, be it good or bad.
- And more! blood feud, blood sport, blood and guts, bloodcurdling, blooded, bloodguilt, blood red, bloodstain, bloodstone, bloodsucker, bloody shirt, bloody-minded, lifeblood, and Bloody Mary.

Blood is symbolic of both LIFE and DEATH.

Blood

- Determines destiny
- Atones for sins. Example: the goblet from which the apostles drank held the symbolic blood of Christ.
- Appeases or placates angry gods
- Saves. The Israelites marked their doors with blood from a slaughtered lamb so that the Spirit of the Lord knew to pass over their homes while on the way to killing first born.
- Destroys
- Heals
- Is lustful passion
- Is rage
- Is violence
- Is an ingredient in witch brews
- Is divine
- Marks one's entry into adulthood. Blood brother rites and/or a woman's first menses
- Contaminates. Some early cultures believed women's monthly blood made them unclean.
- Drinking blood was one way to absorb the power of your enemies.
- Bloodletting, in all its ancient and modern forms

- Brings emotional trauma or pain
- A favorite of vampires everywhere
- Purifies and corrupts
- Saves and curses
- Doesn't wash off. See Lady Macbeth for details.
- Incriminates and exonerates

An example from Shakespeare

"Who would have thought the old man had so much blood in him?" Lady Macbeth says this after helping Macbeth kill King Duncan and as she's washing her hands of the blood she hallucinates on her hands.

It has nothing to do with the amount of blood in his body but rather is symbolic of:

- The lasting legacy of Duncan's good stewardship
- Duncan's bloodline (his sons)
- Lady Macbeth's guilt
- The emotional pain King Duncan's death brought the kingdom
- Macbeth's killing spree
- Macbeth's destruction of the kingdom

Have a bloody good time bleeding life and death into your characters.

TEN

BODY

The body is a temple. We've heard the expression. And everybody knows a temple is a place of worship and a place to access the divine. Even Apostle Paul said, "Do you not know that your body is a temple of the Holy Spirit, who is in you, whom you have received from God?" (1 Cor. 6:19-20).

It should come as no surprise that our body parts hold ancient symbolic meanings. So before fixating on a character's body part you might want to explore the symbolism associated with it, in case you want to give your story some symbolic *zing*.

Head

- Most important part because reason, wisdom, intellect, and spirituality reside within
- Equated with authority and power (heads

of state, heads of corporations)
- A bowed head is a sign of respect.
- Tilts, nods, or shakes are powerful communicators.
- Many-headed gods depicted different aspects or personalities. Shiva, Hecate, Brahma, and Janus have multiple heads.

CONSIDERATIONS

▸ Does your character have a big head? It may denote arrogance or intellect.

▸ Does your character have a small head? It may denote their small mindedness or simple mindedness.

▸ Does your character get knocked on the head and get sense knocked into or out of them?

Hair

- Divine power and virility
- Inner and physical toughness. When Delilah snipped Samson's tresses, she reduced his physical strength.
- Cutting the hair was a sign of sacrifice or surrender. In modern times, if done by a

woman, the act symbolizes rebellion or liberation from feminine gender roles/expectations.

- Mary Magdalene's long flowing hair was a sign of immoral sexual behavior.

Ears

- Equated with a seashell or a spiral.
- Associated with birth. Karma was born from his mother's ear.
- Long ears are linked to wisdom in Buddhism.
- The satyr's large, pointed ears reflect his sexual and sensual nature.

Nose

- Knowing
- Intrusiveness or meddlesome behavior/personality
- Valued by early man as a way of finding food.
- A phallic symbol
- A nose that grows in length indicates a lie, courtesy of Pinocchio.
- A turned-up nose displays contempt.

Mouth

- Deemed the creative force, but it's our mouths which can get us in trouble.
- The Mouth of Hell devours the wicked.
- Articulates our heart's desires.
- Just slap a big X-rated sign on the lips

CONSIDERATIONS

▸ Is the size of your character's mouth an indicator of whether they have a voice in the world?

Tongue/Teeth

- Symbolic of speech
- Visible manifestation of the spoken word
- Teeth are symbolic of animalistic strength and aggression.
- Long teeth are a sign of ambition. Agrippina, Nero's ambitious mother, had double canines.
- The tongue is either a destroyer or a creator.
- Sticking one's tongue out harkens back to times when that gesture warded off evil spirits

Shoulders

- Strength. Think Atlas holding up the world.
- Power
- Carrying responsibilities

CONSIDERATIONS

▸ Do your character's broad shoulders denote his ability to shoulder responsibility?

Skeleton

- Harbinger of death
- Bones symbolize strength, stability, and determination.
- Chakras, the body's energy forces, are aligned with the spine.

CONSIDERATIONS

▸ Does your character stand up straight? Slump? Hunch? Does it indicate their fortitude or outlook on life?

Organs

- Intestines are symbolic of long life and eternity.
- Intestines were used for divination in early times.
- The spleen is where melancholy and laughter come from (part of the ol' 4 Humors of the Body theory)
- The liver symbolized passion during ancient Roman times.

Limbs

- Balance
- Movement
- Good luck
- Arms are symbolic of strength, power, protection, and justice.

Hands

- Command
- Protect
- Bless/bestow
- Pledge and promise
- Symbolize power and strength
- Teach
- Heal

- The omnipotent Hand of God
- The Hamsa hand is a protective talisman used by Muslims and Jews to protect against the evil eye.

Handy Phrases

Hand in hand, firsthand, in hand, hands off, glad hand, hand to mouth, old hand, on one hand, hand-picked, helping hands, at hand, off hand, hand over, hand over fist, hand in glove, back hand, hand me down, free hand, hand to hand, right hand man, hand-picked, iron hand, by the hand, and many, many more.

CONSIDERATIONS

▸ What size are your characters' hands? Large hands may denote their ability to handle things.

▸ Or, conversely, to take things away.

▸ Strong hands may denote strength in handling things or the ability to brutalize.

▸ Are your character's hands smooth and soft? Rough and chapped? Arthritic? Elegant? Old and gnarled? Youthful? Plump? Scarred? Adorned with rings? Tattooed?

All these may act as subtle indicators of their personality.

As expressive communicators, we are familiar with the meanings of:

- Palms out
- Finger pointing to heaven
- Handshakes
- Hand wringing
- Hand washing (Pontius Pilate and Lady Macbeth)
- Hidden hands denote respect in Asian cultures, but mistrust in western.

Gender-Specific Body Part

Early man was obsessed with those particular parts. Wait, we still are!

Male

- Strength
- Power
- Virility

Female

- Regeneration
- Fertility
- Procreation
- Miracle of birth

Feet

- Mobility
- Rooted or in touch with self and nature
- Bare feet touching the ground is man's link to the Divine Earth.
- The monk's bare feet signify their vow of poverty.
- In Asian cultures, feet are considered unclean so it's wrong to display soles to another.
- Solid foundation
- Washing another's feet is a symbol of hospitality and humility.
- The Buddha's footprint found at Buddhist temples indicates the Buddha's presence.

As you can see, lots of body parts were left out. This is just the tip of the body iceberg. A quick Google search will reveal many more symbolic aspects.

What symbolic body part needs to be emphasized for your character?

ELEVEN

EYES

Eyes are powerful symbols. The mere glance glimmer gawk gaze ogle glare bore focus beam sparkle peek peer look goggle gape leer (did I miss any?) reveals a character's emotions.

No wonder the eyes are the windows of the soul. But there's more to eyes than...well, meets the eye.

Ancient Eyes

- The Right Eye of Horus. God. Wadjet (the falcon-headed god associated with the Eye of Ra.) They are all about protection, royal power, and health.
- The Left Eye of Horus represents the moon. Shown together, they represent the entire universe.
- The Third Eye or ajna (the brow chakra)

is associated with spiritual sight, enlightenment, or a heightened state of awareness/consciousness. It's the eye used by clairvoyants, mediums, psychics, and seers.

- The Eye of Providence or the all-seeing eye of God, is often depicted enclosed by a triangle (the trinity) with emanating rays of light signifying God's omnipresence and omnipotence.

- The Evil Eye describes someone looking at someone with hatred, envy, or malevolence. The greatest injury is to those who do not know the Evil Eye is aimed at them, thereby allowing negative energy to permeate their bodies and souls. To counter this, people wore amulets to deflect these cursed stares.

Eyes are symbolic of:

- Enlightenment
- Knowledge
- Wisdom
- Discernment
- Spirituality

In Greek Myths

- Cyclopes had one eye, which suggests he did not have the wisdom or self-awareness of the humans he enjoyed terrorizing.
- The eye on a peacock's feathers indicates humankind's penchant for being overly concerned with appearances and the external world. Goddess Hera tossed the giant Argos' 100 eyes (he only closed a few at a time when sleeping) onto the bird's feathers.

Eye Color:

Does the color of a character's eyes matter? Maybe.

- Brown eyes are opaque and seen as less emotional and more ordinary.
- Black eyes are deemed evil or cold-hearted or, conversely, their emotions are of a fathomless depth.
- Blue eyes are associated with emotional and/or ethereal qualities, perhaps they appear more transparent, and thus we believe we can see into their soul. Blue eyes are associated with the water and sky, two divine and mysterious elements. It's also easier for others to see pupil

dilation in a blue-eyed person, which we know indicates emotion.

- Green eyes are deemed mysterious, exotic, magical, and are often equated with witches and sorcery.

Eyes, no matter what color, may be described as:

- Cold: unemotional
- Hard: uncaring
- Warm: kind
- Soft: loving and affectionate
- Watery/cloudy: stricken with overwhelming emotion
- Deep: harboring secrets or unexpressed emotion
- Sparkling: excited, anticipatory, happy, and/or smitten
- Dilated: indicating sexual arousal or drug use
- Glowing: creepy, of the netherworld, evil, or divine and celestial
- Bright: keen, intelligent, curious
- Sharp: accusatory, wary
- Wide: wonder, amazement, incredulity
- Blank: devoid of emotion, sociopathic, zombie-like

A Word About Blindness

In literature, blindness is equated with wisdom. Prophets (like Tiresias) in Greek plays are blind. They see with their hearts the truth in an event, character, or circumstance. Visual seeing is *not* believing. When Oedipus blinds himself after discovering he fulfilled the prophecy he tried to avoid, the reader understands the symbolic nature of his act. A more current example is Neo in *The Matrix*. In the final movie, he no longer needs to see, his inner sight/intuition/conscious the only sense he needs to "see" the truth. Another fun movie that "focuses" on eyes and is rife with eye symbolism is *Equilibrium*.

Have fun seeing your characters with new eyes!

TWELVE

COLOR

I bet you can rattle off four different songs that have a color in the title. That's because color is attached to a spectrum of emotions. Savvy writers know color can symbolize, reveal, and add irony. Color symbolism is fraught with ambiguity and duality, making it a vibrant way to add complexity.

Warm colors like yellow, red, and orange are considered stimulating.

The **cool colors** of blue, indigo, and violet are soothing and peaceful.

Remember, color symbolism varies with culture

Red: a dual-tinted mix

- Passion and lust
- Anger and aggression
- War and revolution
- Fire and flame

- All these emotions spur one to action.
- The red planet Mars is named after the Roman god of war.
- Associated with the root chakra located at the base of the spine, our connection with the earth.

Yellow: the good side

- Sun and gold (metal)
- Enlightenment and wisdom
- Flowers and warmth
- Associated with the solar plexus chakra

Yellow: the bad side

- Cowardliness
- Envy and treachery

Orange: a mix of the first two

- Luxury and splendor
- A renunciation of earthly pleasures. Example: a Buddhist monk's garb
- Associated with the sacral chakra, the reproductive organs.
- In ancient Rome, a bride wore a saffron-colored wrap and an orange veil.

Blue has as many hues as meanings.

- Sky and infinity
- The divine. The Egyptian god Amun and Hindu gods, Rama, Shiva, and Krishna are blue.
- Tranquility and reflection
- Intellect
- Depression
- Sexual proclivities. Example: blue movies
- Socio-economic status, from blue-collar to blue blood
- In Egypt, blue was the color of truth.
- The Virgin Mary's blue robe signifies her purity.
- Indigo is the color of the brow, or third eye chakra of spiritual knowing and intuition.

Green

- Spring and new life
- Fertility and nature
- Youth and inexperience
- Hope and joy
- Envy and jealousy
- Decay

- Connected with safeguarding our planet's resources promoted by the Green Movement
- Associated with the heart chakra

Purple/Violet

- Royalty and wealth
- Luxury
- Power. Roman senators were identified by the purple stripe on their togas.
- Religion. Catholic clergy don purple vestments during Advent and Lent.
- Associated with the bliss, oneness, serenity, and spiritual wisdom of the crown chakra.
- Temperance, because it's a mixture of red (action & heat) and blue (calm & cool)

Pink

- Femininity
- Baby girls

Black

- Evil or darkness

- Despair, death, and mourning
- Mortality
- Secrecy
- Ill-fortune
- Disease

Gray, in all its many shades

- Gloom
- Anonymity, inconspicuousness, or namelessness
- Old age
- Uncertainty, unreliability, and risk

White

- Purity and innocence. Brides and those being baptized are clothed in white.
- Goodness
- Holiness
- In China, Japan, and India, white is associated with death and mourning.
- Surrender and peace

CONSIDERATIONS

▸ Although folks may not know the exact symbolic aspects of a color, they do get a gut feeling. If your protagonist's debut appearance is in a white dress, readers will see that as a portrayal of innocence. Even if the character isn't. Be mindful of color and all it may imply.

THIRTEEN

COLOR DESCRIPTORS

Does your character wear a red dress? What shade of red? Red, beyond the western symbolism of lust, power, and anger, offers a few clues to the reader. But you can give it a symbolic nudge by including the shade of red.

- A rose-colored dress conveys ladylikeness or love.
- A cherry-red dress is suggestive of sexual prowess or desire, or, *ahem*…a woman wishing to be deflowered.
- An apple-red dress suggests something forbidden or idyllic.
- A blood-red dress…well, when you mix two symbolic words you get a metaphoric punch in the symbolic face!

- A woman with ruby lips is sultry and/or high maintenance.
- A woman with candy-apple lips sounds like a fun time.

You've all seen the meme dismissing color symbolism (and literary analysis) and yet consider this, a fabric described as *bone* evokes a much different emotion than one described as *snow*.

CONSIDERATIONS

▸ Genre: Sweet romance novels might use more romantic colors. Example: caramel—sweet and gooey, like love—instead of light brown.

▸ Historical fiction authors need to be mindful of using color names that didn't exist in that century. A lipstick-red dress won't work if there was no lipstick back then. You're better off using a descriptor like *ruby*.

Revealing Character

Is your character a murderer? He/she might see their color world in shades of viscera. A gardener or florist may see their world in terms of blooms and flora. A chef or a woman on a diet might describe the world with food colors.

- Jewel tones convey preciousness, worth, or rarity.
- Nature colors convey the idyllic.
- There are city colors and farmland colors, youthful and aged colors, fun colors, mysterious colors, clean colors and dirty colors, evil colors and good colors.

FOURTEEN

WHAT NOTS

A person's home is their castle. It's also chockfull of symbolic furnishings and doodads. Give your story some symbolic *zing* by being familiar with a few of the household symbolic heavyweights.

Book: Wisdom and Learning

CONSIDERATIONS

▸ Is the book old or new?
▸ Are pages dog-eared or torn out
(think *Dead Poet's Society*)?
▸ Is the print large or small?
▸ Does the book need a translation?
▸ Does the book contain esoteric, forbidden,
or dangerous information? Remember the
movie, *The Mummy,* when the Egyptologist
yells, "You must not read from the book!"

Bowl: Equated with the feminine. It's a womb thing. And also, prosperity. Get it? A full bowl versus an empty bowl says a lot about the character and/or their circumstances.

CONSIDERATIONS

▸ Is the bowl full or empty?
▸ What are the contents?
▸ What material is it made from?

Box: The unconscious mind. Think Pandora. Containment of emotions. Limitations. Close-mindedness.

CONSIDERATIONS

▸ Is the box open or closed?
▸ Is it locked?
▸ What is the box made of?
▸ Where is the box kept?
▸ Who opens the box?
▸ Who locks the box?

Broom: Spiritual cleaning. Ridding home of evil. Protection against curses. Witch transportation.

CONSIDERATIONS

‣ Who is sweeping?

‣ What problem is swept away?

‣ Is the broom constructed from a specific and therefore symbolic wood?

Fan: Femininity. Social class. Dispels evil spirits. Releases soul into immortal realm (Taoism).

CONSIDERATIONS

‣ Who holds the fan?

‣ How is it used? To cool, hide, flirt, conceal?

Hearth: Home. Family. Emotional warmth. Females. Maternal nurturing.

CONSIDERATIONS

‣ Is the fire smoldering, blazing, or put out?

‣ Who is tending the fire?

▸ Who is the beneficiary of the warmth?

▸ What is burning? A romantic or incrimi-
nating letter, a body, evidence?

▸ How big is the fireplace?

▸ Is the hearth ornate or simple? Luxurious,
pretentious, or utilitarian?

Key: Access to wisdom. Freedom. Success. Secrets. Two crossed keys are a Christian emblem of the Gates of Heaven.

CONSIDERATIONS

▸ What is the key made of?

▸ Who is using the key?

▸ Why is the door locked?

▸ Does the key work in the door?

▸ Who and why does someone steal the key?

Knife: Death.   Sacrifice.   Cutting   away emotions/ideals/prejudices/etc.

CONSIDERATIONS

▸ Who is wielding the blade?

> ▸ What is being cut?
> ▸ Is the blade dull or sharp?

Looms: Mother Goddess. Luna goddess. Feminine power.

CONSIDERATIONS

> ▸ Who is weaving?
> ▸ What pattern is created?
> ▸ What colors are woven?
> ▸ What material is used?

Mirror: A million meanings, well, almost. Vanity. Truth. Clarity. Distortion. Reflection of soul. Inner calm (Taoists).   Transitory   nature   of   reality (Hinduism).

CONSIDERATIONS

> ▸ Who or what is reflected?
> ▸ What is *not* reflected?
> ▸ How is the mirror framed?
> ▸ Does the mirror break? And if so,
> what *really* broke inside of the character?

Pen & Ink: Learning. Creativity. Destiny.

CONSIDERATIONS

▸ What is written?
▸ Who is the writer?
▸ Does the writer make mistakes or blot the paper?
▸ Is the script illegible, elegant, precise?
▸ What surface is it written on?

Purse: Wealth. Vanity. Prosperity.

CONSIDERATIONS

▸ Is the purse full or empty?
▸ What material is the purse? Remember, you can't make a silk purse from a sow's ear.

Screen: Mystery. Concealment.

CONSIDERATIONS

▸ Who is behind the screen? Is it titillating or frightening?

▸ Who is looking at the person/thing behind the screen?

▸ What material is the screen made of? Sheer or thick?

Table: The Last Supper. Equality, if it's round. A coming together. Circle of Life. The Divine.

CONSIDERATIONS

▸ What shape is the table?
▸ What material is it made from?
▸ Who sits at the head of the table?
▸ Who arrives and who leaves?
▸ Is something spilled on the table?

Thread: One's lifetime as determined by the gods.

CONSIDERATIONS

▸ Who cuts the thread?
▸ What material is the thread? Coarse wool or silk?

▸ What is the thread stitching together?

▸ Did the thread become loose?

Timepiece: Mortality

CONSIDERATIONS

▸ Does the clock run fast, slow, or exact?

▸ Does someone stop time?

▸ Is time more important for one character than another?

FIFTEEN

CLOTHING

Sometimes clothing matters. Sometimes it doesn't. It's a detail to be sure. Many newbie writers include long descriptive passages about clothing that ultimately do not matter, don't add to characterization, add irony, or foreshadow anything.

A word or two can convey a lot about a character's emotion, intent, and personality. Recall *The Devil Wears Prada*? The clothing and appearance of the characters spoke volumes! Clothes can reveal culture, socio-economic status, personality, profession, age, emotion, and more.

A sentence like, *John tossed his gray Armani suit jacket over the chair and propped up his feet, scuffed shoes and all, on the desk* suggest John's: 1) lack of attention to detail; 2) falling on hard times; 3) being a man of opposites. This one sentence may be one of many characterization clues about John.

Just as we make snap judgments about someone's appearance, correct or not, clothing reveals or hides clues about your character.

Clothing may be:

- wrinkled or pressed
- scuffed or polished (shoes, jewelry)
- designer or fake
- casual or dressy
- business or athletic
- cheap or expensive
- severe or flirty
- trendy, classic, or outdated
- sedate or flashy
- oversized, form-fitting, or tight
- bright or somber colors
- patterned or plain
- ill-fitting or custom

What do your characters' clothes reveal about their personality?

SIXTEEN

FIRE & WATER

These are symbolic powerhouses. Their meanings stem from a myriad of religious beliefs, legends, and myths. Fire and water represent a universe of power, destruction, ambiguity, duality, and divinity. Whether earthly or otherworldly, these forces of nature are feared and loved with equal fervor. No wonder authors love playing with their multiple meanings in poetry and literature.

Fire

- War and chaos
- Linked to the sun or lightning
- Associated with passion, creativity, anger, or wrath
- Method of purification
- A way to regenerate. The Phoenix rises from the ashes.

- Knowledge. Prometheus brought fire to people and suffered grievously for it.
- Violence and destruction
- God's glory. Moses and the burning bush or the flaming hearts of Christianity.
- Elevated us above the animals
- Eternal flame above an altar
- Flames of hell

Fire Gods & Creatures

- Vulcan: Roman god associated with volcanoes and craftsmanship, since weapons and tools are forged from fire.
- Chu Jung: Chinese god who punished those who broke heavenly laws.
- Chantico: Aztec goddess of the hearth and volcanoes, and the patroness for goldsmiths.
- Sekhmet: A woman (usually) with a lioness's head. This Egyptian god killed enemies with arrows of fire and kept a fire-spewing snake at her side.
- Agni: Vedic god (means *fire* in Sanskrit) is often depicted with two heads indicating both his merciful and destructive nature.
- Maui: a Polynesian god who stole fire from the Earth mother.

- Ifrit: Not a god, but an Arabic and Islamic supernatural creature of fire who is usually portrayed as evil.
- Salamander: Also not a god, but one of the four elementals.

Water

- Divine wrath. Almost every religion has a version of the flood story.
- Transformative
- Changeable, from stagnant to raging, from shallow to deep
- Destroys
- Purifies. Baptism is an example.
- Primordial. All life sprang forth from its ooze in many creation myths.
- Life-giving. Example: the Fountain of Youth.
- Fertility and irrigation
- Natural and symbolic barrier to another place or realm
- Reflecting, although it led to Narcissus' drowning
- Method of transition to the next life
- Method of torture
- Divination
- Healing
- Four Rivers of Paradise

- The river Styx separates Earth from
  Hades
- Sacred, from Holy Water to the Ganges.

Water Gods & Creatures

- Poseidon/Neptune: trident-bearing god
  who rides upon dolphins and controls
  the seas
- Sedna: Inuit sea goddess rules over all
  sea creatures
- Charybdis: Monster-daughter of
  Poseidon who takes the form of a
  whirlpool that sucks in unsuspecting
  sailors
- Mermaids/selkies
- Encantado: dolphin shape-shifter and
  seducer of humankind
- Undines. One of the four Elementals.
- Nereids
- Sirens
- And Mami Wata, Jengus, Makaras,
  Hippocamps, Bunyips, Adaros, Kappas,
  Grindylows, Bishop Fish, Cetus,
  Kraken…and I probably missed quite
  a few!

SEVENTEEN

MORE WATER

Authors may use rain or a dunk in the water to indicate a character's spiritual change or spiritual rebirth… good or bad.

A character may:

- dance in the rain, indicating joy at their new lease on life.
- jump in a lake/pond/river/ocean/pool of their own accord, signifying a *determined* effort to change.
- be pushed or dragged into a lake/pond/river/ocean/pool, which may indicate their *unwillingness* to change.
- emerge as bad/evil. Think about what happened to the Joker in *Batman* who falls into the vat of acid.

- accidentally slips or trips into the water signifying a less purposeful change.

CONSIDERATIONS

▸ Is the water polluted?

▸ Does the character float on his back and gaze at the sky, which may suggest confidence and limitless possibilities?

▸ Does the character struggle or get tangled in seaweed?

▸ Is the character dragged down by their possessions?

▸ Is the water warm or cold or arctic?

▸ Does someone save the character?

▸ Does the character refuse to be saved?

▸ Does the character save himself?

▸ Is the body of water religiously significant?

Water can be a plot device or something more.

EIGHTEEN

ILLNESS

Do you need to kill one of your darlings? Illness provides an opportunity to reveal a character's:

- flaws or weaknesses
- last thoughts
- emotional/psychological/spiritual growth

Diseases can be:

- horrifyingly ugly and/or painful
- tragic
- picturesque
- mysterious
- the result of divine wrath
- a plot device
- ironic

A **weak heart** or heart attack can symbolize a character's:

- heartlessness
- having too much heart/compassion
- broken heart

Cancer may be:

- a manifestation of a personality trait.
- emotional damage inflicted by others.
- a metaphor. Example: a character with brain cancer may reveal someone who thinks too much, not enough, or has a deeply flawed viewpoint.
- a metaphor for a character's proclivities, flaws, or strengths.

Seizures may reveal:

- a character's inability to control their emotions
- physical manifestation of the thrashing received from society/group/individual

Auto immune disease is today's tragic illness. It may symbolize a character who is not immune to the emotional hurt inflicted by society/culture/other characters.

Ebola & other hemorrhagic fevers may suggest a character's emotional "bleeding."

Bone disorders or back problems can reflect a character's having "no backbone" or being weak willed (bones symbolize strength).

Rabies may be symbolic of a character's repressed hostility and aggressiveness.

Leprosy would surely indicate some kind of Biblical divine wrath.

Vision problems may reflect a character's inability to see the truth.

Have fun killing your characters!

NINETEEN

LIGHT & DARK

These two little words are fraught with BIG symbolic meaning. We know the obvious. The Light of Knowledge and the Darkness of the Soul, but writers can use darkness and light in a myriad of ways.

Light may refer to:

- Goodness
- Enlightenment, from the prosaic to the sublime
- Divinity/cosmic power
- Morality
- Truth
- Vitality/youth
- Innocence
- Spirituality

- An attitude, emotion, or personality unencumbered with worries
- Imagination/creativity/inspiration
- Joy

Darkness may refer to:

- Evil
- Corruption/degradation/baseness
- Netherworld/underworld
- Lies/falseness
- Guilt
- Sin
- Ignorance, in all its many forms
- Mystery
- Fear
- An attitude, emotion, or personality fraught with misery or ill will
- Grief
- Tainted or impure thoughts

Light and dark symbolism can:

- Describe a character's mood or personality
- Foreshadow a character's intent
- Foreshadow an event
- Indicate a setting's moral/ethical beliefs
- Reveal irony

- Provide moral/ethical/religious contrast between opposing characters/themes/events
- Be a plot device
- Be symbolic
- Be a theme
- Be a recurring motif

TWENTY

SEX

Intercourse. Coupling. Hanky-panky. Horizontal mambo. Lovemaking. Copulation. Fornication. Coitus. Carnal Knowledge. To know. Relations.

That's a small sampling of synonyms. Each provokes a different emotional reaction by virtue of its connotation. As you may imagine, there are many reasons why sex scenes are included in a novel. Writing a sex scene is tricky. There's a wide range of spice levels, from G to X-rated.

Ask yourself:

- Why is the sex scene there? Is it advancing the plot?
- How is it advancing the plot?
- Is it gratuitous? (erotica)
- Is the sex scene about something other than sex?

- Is the sex scene a metaphor or symbolic of a character's emotional growth or downfall?
- Is the sex scene symbolic for the characters' relationship?
- Is it thematic?

Sex

- Reveals emotional/societal/cultural/phycological relationships between characters
- Foreshadows a change in a relationship
- Reveals a character's emotional state.
- Can be a plot device

CONSIDERATIONS

▸ Is character allowing themselves emotional/physical pleasure?

▸ Is their non-pleasure of the act symbolic of their inability to be intimate or let go?

▸ Is the character using sex for selfish purposes?

▸ Is the character sacrificing themselves sexually for a cause/purpose, be it honorable or not?

▸ Is the character using sex to rebel against

cultural/family/gender/societal/ expectations
or rules?

▶ If the act is especially taboo, what is the
character's motivation or reason?

▶ Is sex symbolic of the character's resigned
attitude toward cultural/family/gender/societal
expectations?

▶ Is the character the aggressor? Passive?
The instigator? Innocent? Experienced?

▶ Is the sex act a metaphor for who's in
control?

▶ Is sex symbolic of their
spiritual/emotional enlightenment?

▶ Is sex a plea? Is the character begging/asking
for love/acceptance/privilege/favor/ their life?

▶ Is sex symbolic of the transcendent or
divine nature of love?

Older Lovers

If an older experienced man or woman is having
sex with a younger naïve person, sex may be a
symbol for:

- Loss of innocence
- Using power or position to exploit
  another

- Blatant disregard for society/people/culture
- Destroying a life
- Corrupting the conquest's morals/values

Taking all the above into account, the challenge is using appropriate language and tone to convey your true purpose (the author's intent) for including sex. Will your description be explicit, flowery, romantic, vague, clinical, or nasty? Be mindful of genre expectations.

TWENTY-ONE

MEALTIME

Oh, the drama of the family meal! People eating and drinking together is tasty with yummy symbolism.

Why is that, you ask? In ancient times, sharing one's meal symbolized hospitality and goodwill. Certain foods, drink, or days were associated with religious and social rituals.

If one was breaking bread with someone, it indicated friendship, truce, partnership, or an alliance. The human race hasn't changed all that much. We still enjoy eating with those we like and eschew eating with those we don't.

Eating and/or fasting rituals are found in most religions. And I can't think of a holiday that doesn't center around food and eating. Or fasting and then eating. Sharing food is an act of agreement, fellowship, and harmony.

Shared meals may:

- Be a plot device
- Reveal character
- Reveal the relationships between characters
- Be thematic
- Be an allusion to other famous religious meals or foods, like the Last Supper
- Be an allusion to famous literary meals

Writing a meal scene is challenging, but can reveal much about the plot, characters, relationships, family dynamics, setting, or culture.

CONSIDERATIONS

▸ Who is sharing the meal? Enemies? Lovers? Family? Strangers?

▸ What foods are they eating? Is the food and drink symbolic of religion or social class?

▸ Is the food itself fraught with symbolism?

▸ Why is the particular meal described? How is it significant to the plot/character?

▸ How does the meal end? Did someone choke? Which may be a plot device or a sign of a character "choking" on their own words or that of another.

▸ Did someone stalk off? That may indicate the relationship went wrong. Remember the scene in *Great Gatsby* when Tom jumps up from the table to take a phone call from his girlfriend?

▸ How is the character eating? Are they nibbling (dainty), gobbling (gluttonous), selective (picky)?

▸ Are they sloppy or neat or overly fastidious?

▸ Did a character stop eating mid meal? Why?

▸ Is a character enjoying their meal with great gusto? Are they smacking their lips, making *mmm* and *ah* and *oh* noises?

▸ How does the character feel about the meal? If they hate trying a new food, it may indicate they are closed-minded. If they enjoy trying new food, it may indicate they are open-minded.

▸ Does a character take food from another's plate? Do they refuse to share?

▸ Does a character become sick? Is it a plot device or is a character "sick of" or "sickened by" a character, conversation, or turn of events at the table?

▸ Is a character eating with his favorite twelve friends? This is an allusion to the Last Supper and foreshadows betrayal.

▸ Do the characters share a utensil, straw, or drink either accidentally or on purpose?

▸ Does one character feed another? This may

be erotic, suggestive, a prelude to sex, or reveal who is the boss in the relationship.

▸ What's happening under the table? Hand-holding? Clenched fists?

▸ Is a character refusing to eat, in effect saying, I'm here with you, but I don't like/approve of you.

An eating scene is full of chewy symbolic deliciousness. Have fun feeding your characters!

TWENTY-TWO

TOPOGRAPHY

Topography is more than just the setting of your novel. It can express theme, plot device, or act as an antagonist.

It may indicate or foreshadow a character's:

- moral growth or decay
- emotion
- problems or dilemmas

Geography and topography can also serve as moral, emotional, intellectual, or spiritual indicators.

Mountains and higher elevations suggest moral righteousness or spiritual awareness. It's the whole closer to god thing. There's a reason why the guru in every joke sits atop a mountain. In *Frankenstein*, the monster leads his creator across the tallest mountains and glaciers in Europe. This is ironic, since both monster and creator are immoral, indignant, murderous, arrogant, and angry. Although the doctor played god when he created the monster, neither character is high-minded nor virtuous enough to do the right thing. It's an ironic and symbolic double whammy.

Steep ground suggests trials and tribulations to surmount. Think *The Sound of Music* song "Climb Every Mountain." It's not a song about hiking but about opportunities.

Flat lands may reveal the "flatness" or dullness of a character's life.

Swamps imply low morals, poverty, lack of faith, a dirty or degraded sense of self, or a connection to the primordial ooze of the earth so to speak. Wait! I know exactly what you're thinking! In *Star Wars*, Luke finds Yoda living in a swamp. Yoda is a master Jedi who did not go to the Dark Side. What's he doing living in a swamp? Well…it could be Lucas throwing some irony into the mix or be a plot device or represent the now disrespected, disregarded state of the Force.

Forests are dark and fraught with danger, implying emotional/spiritual/moral ignorance or heading into a place of emotional/spiritual/moral danger. In *Effi Briest,* the two lovers take the *low road* into the *dark forest* only moments before the married protagonist decides to have an affair. It's like being hit in the head with a symbolic 2 by 4.

Vegetable gardens suggest practicality, abundance, frugality, and health, but not necessarily fertility.

Orchards, depending on the fruit or nut, is associated with fertility, abundance, and prosperity.

Deserts hint at a character's hopes and dreams drying up or they have become an emotional/spiritual/moral wasteland.

Jungles are dangerous and contain scantily clad heathens. Expect some loosening of morals or spiritual soul searching or primitive behavior.

Caves, as Plato's *Allegory of the Cave* suggests, is all about shadows vs reality and philosophical enlightenment. Yes, I know, a total over-simplification.

Cliffs. Remember the Cliffs of Insanity in *Princess Bride*? Precipices shout DANGER! A character or sentiment or perception or judgement or insight or truth is going over the edge—dashed to bits by the rocks below. If you have a cliff in your novel, put it to good symbolic use.

An **urban setting** may indicate the story's fast-paced cosmopolitan complex plot or the character's urban lifestyle or serve as a sharp contrast to either.

Small town or **rural settings** tell a reader the plot will be charming, cozy or small town creepy or serve as irony.

CONSIDERATIONS

▸ What is the topography revealing about the character's morals, emotions, intellect or spirit?

▸ Is the topography hindering or helping them?

▸ Is the topography representative of their struggles?

Take some advice from realtors. It's all about location, location, location!

TWENTY-THREE

WEATHER

Weather is more than the change of atmospheric conditions. It's fraught with symbolism, especially bad weather. Be careful! It's easy to overdo and become trite and cliché.

Need to portend a change? Use weather.

- The **crack of thunder** can happen after a character's ominous or foreboding or creepy statement.
- **Gathering rain clouds** signal the brewing emotional storm for the characters.
- **Rain, thunder, and lightning** suggests a bit of divine wrath or judgement is coming your character's way.
- **Bad weather** in every Shakespearean

play signifies "something wicked this way comes."

Rain may be:

- a plot device
- an emotion or spiritual cleansing or healing
- a character's drowning with despair
- a metaphor for tearful emotions, happy or sad
- a new life/new beginning/new outlook

CONSIDERATIONS

▸ Is the rain gently sprinkling or pouring buckets?

▸ Is it raining WATER? Because in Haruki Murakami's *Kafka on the Shore*, it rains fish.

▸ A freezing cold rain might mean the character's spiritual rebirth is one of heartlessness or they become numb to their emotional pain.

▸ A fresh spring rain symbolizes a fresh start or rebirth of life.

▸ Does the character have an umbrella? Is their face lifted to the sky, or do they protect themselves with a heavy raincoat?

▸ Are they "singing in the rain?"

▸ Do they become splattered with mud?

Another symbolic smack in the face, the mud suggesting their life/situation spotting/soiling/ruining their new spiritual/emotional cleansing.

Snow

- Light, fluffy flakes are symbolic of happiness and romance and good will toward men. Are you having flashbacks of every sappy Christmas movie you ever saw?
- A snowstorm that traps characters can mirror their own entrapment or be the perfect set up for a horror or romance story.

Fog

- indicates confusion.
- The character is "in a fog" about their life, a relationship, or a problem.
- In Mary Shelley's *Frankenstein*, Dr. Frankenstein tracks the monster in thick fog. The more obsessive he becomes, the more fog. Dr. Frankenstein loses his way both psychologically and morally, the

fog acting as an atmospheric indicator of
both his murky morals and the darkness
of his soul.

Before writing "it was a dark and stormy night,"
consider the implications of the weather.

TWENTY-FOUR

VIOLENCE

BaM! SmAcK! PoW! Violence! We love it! In many genres, it's 100% necessary.

Violence may be:

- **thematic**: Think *Fight Club, The Old Testament, Heart of Darkness, The Things They Carried,* or *Persepolis.*
- **biblical**: Wrestling with an angel (Jacob wrestling with Metatron) or the Crucifixion of Jesus or a devastating flood
- **Shakespearean**: "Tis not so deep as a well, nor as wide as a church door, but 'tis enough, 'twill serve. Ask for me tomorrow and you shall find a grave man." Mercutio to Romeo after Tybalt

stabs him. "Et tu, Brute?" Caesar after Brutus stabs him.

- **allegorical**: The stoning or just the whole darn story in Shirley Jackson's "The Lottery."
- **transcendent:** The flames of passion engulfing the two lovers in Laura Esquivel's *Like Water for Chocolate.*
- **metaphoric**: Violence is equated with masculinity in Chinua Achebe's *Things Fall Apart.*
- **a plot device**: Most action-adventure movies.
- **symbolic**: In *God of Small Things*, a character is beaten to a bloody pulp by the police. It's symbolic of: 1) the injustice of India's caste system; 2) the consequences of disregarding cultural taboos; and 3) the cost of true love in a racist society.
- **gratuitous**: What can I say? Some of us need a little BAM! POW! BASH!

CONSIDERATIONS

▶ The **proximity** of the two adversaries. The closer they are, the more intimate (personal) the violence.

▶ The **location** where the violence occurs. A

fight in a church has different implications than a fight in the forest.

▸ **Weaponry**: Buffy the Vampire Slayer kills demons with a wooden stake. That's classic old school!

▸ The **evilness** of the bad guy. Does the Bad Guy/Gal get his comeuppance or is his less-than-painful death a symbol/metaphor for some point you're making about culture/humanity/religion/gender/etc.

▸ What body part delivers the hit? Fist, leg, knee, hand, finger, head, elbow? A knee to the groin is ever so much nastier than a fist to the nose.

▸ What **body part** takes the hits? A gal's cutting a guy's man part off is very symbolic.

▸ We all know what a stab in the back means. Hits from behind are associated with cowardice.

▸ Frontal attacks are usually equated with courage.

Have fun terrorizing your characters!

TWENTY-FIVE

NATURE

Plants and trees and all things nature may be used in a variety of literary ways.

Nature can be a:

- Metaphor
- Symbol
- Foreshadowing device
- Allusion
- Plot device
- Characterization device

CONSIDERATIONS

▸ **Blooms**

▸ Flowering suggests a blossoming or awakening of a character's personality, intellect, morals, understanding, love etc.

▸ **Dried/Dead/Wilted**
▸ Metaphoric or symbolic suggestion of something, like an idea, problem, conflict, ideology, morality, opinion, or attitude that is dead or dying
▸ May foreshadow a character's demise
▸ Characterize an aspect of something that is dead/destroyed within a character's soul or heart

▸ **New Growth**
▸ Denotes new beginnings, fresh starts, renewal, or hope *unless*…
▸ The growth is deleterious or harmful

▸ **Uprooted**
▸ May convey the root of a problems coming to the surface
▸ Reveal the unearthing of a problem or situation
▸ Characterize the importance of a character's culture

▸ **Yellowed or drying leaves**
▸ Indicates or foreshadows that a character or situation is dying
▸ Suggests the approaching end of one's life or goals or hope

▸ Thorns
▸ A tricky or hurtful/thorny problem or situation
▸ Characterizes a person's prickly/thorny temperament
▸ Foreshadows problems

▸ Shrubbery
▸ Reveals a character's personality
▸ Foreshadows
▸ Hedges enclosing a space may reveal the boundaries of a character or situation
▸ Does the character leap over them? Crash into them? Trip over them? Plant them? Tend to them? Cut them down? Trample them?
▸ Thorny, thick, invasive, wild, sculpted, or overgrown plants may indicate the type of problem/conflict.

▸ Gardens
▸ May be a biblical allusion to the Garden of Eden
▸ Symmetry suggests beauty and a well-rounded intellect
▸ Consider what's in the garden. Plants? Rock garden? Cacti? Statuary? Fruit trees? Vegetables? Flowers? Herbs?
▸ Is it well-tended, wild, gone to seed, in ruin, or meticulous?

▸ Is it a secret garden?

▸ **Trees**
▸ Gnarled limbs may reveal a complex problem
▸ Hint at the strength or weakness of a character
▸ Suggests the strength of a character's heritage/culture
▸ Is the type of tree symbolic? Magical? Biblical?
▸ Indicates soaring ambitions
▸ Does the character climb or swing from its branches?
▸ Do they denote character like the "Four Skinny Trees" chapter found in *House on Mango Street* by Sandra Cisneros?
▸ Does the trunk bend with the wind? Is it stunted? Does it overshadow other trees?

▸ **Meadows**
▸ Pastoral or idyllic atmosphere, unless its full of zombies or raptors
▸ Wild beauty

▸ **Moor**
▸ Think Bronte
▸ Desolate and dreary but can be tragically romantic

‣ Something to be crossed

‣ A great place to ponder one's life

‣ Add fog for some Gothic-style brooding

‣ Vines

‣ Are invasive, take over, and often obscure or smother other plants. Does a character or culture or conflict encroach upon your character?

‣ Flowers

‣ Do they have thorns?

‣ What's the symbolism behind the species?

‣ Are they wilted?

‣ Are they common? Read the short story *Chrysanthemums* by John Steinbeck for a symbolism-packed flower.

‣ Are they exotic like the very symbolic and tattoo-favorite lotus flower?

‣ Is it the red rose of love or is it the "Sick Rose" of William Blake's evocative poem?

‣ Does it grow with others? Or is it a single triumphant daisy growing from a crack in the pavement?

‣ Are the blooms wilted? Or have the buds been nipped off?

‣ Weeds

‣ Unwanted and ugly unless…

▸ They're beautiful weeds, in which case they suggest the beauty in something unwanted and ugly.

▸ Are they a metaphor for a character's persistent problems?

▸ Are they a symbol for the character's troubles in life?

▸ Does the character try to get rid of them or let them take over?

▸ Wide Paths

▸ The physical, spiritual, intellectual, psychological, moral choice is easy.

▸ A common or frequent choice.

▸ Narrow Paths

▸ The physical, spiritual, intellectual, psychological, or moral choice is difficult.

▸ An uncommon or infrequent choice. Example: *The Road Not Taken* by Robert Frost.

▸ Streams and Ponds

▸ Pastoral and charming…usually

▸ Lakes

▸ Can be large or small, cold, frozen, fraught with danger, or harbor giant brontosaurus-type creatures.

▸ In the 1999 movie *Lake Placid*, the idyllic

lake is anything but placid. Can you say irony?

▸ **Rivers**
▸ How fast is the water moving?
▸ Is it the complex symbol found in *Huck Finn* where the Mississippi divides the racist east from the wide-open west, and where direction denotes bias, and is the only place where Jim and Huck are free from prejudiced eyes?
▸ Is it "The Bitter River" of the poem by Langston Hughes?
▸ Is it the river from *Fahrenheit 451* where Montag jumps in to save his life and it symbolizes his intellectual rebirth?

▸ **Gates**
▸ Like all doors, arches, and entry ways, gates signify movement from one realm— physical, spiritual, intellectual, psychological, moral—to another.
▸ Is the gate connected to a white picket fence?
▸ Is the gate wide (easy to go through) or narrow (difficult)?
▸ Is the gate fancy or plain? Ancient or new?

▸ **Bridges**

‣ Connectors of two different physical, spiritual, intellectual, psychological, moral, cultural worlds

‣ Impassable bridges therefore reveal the schism or rift between the two.

‣ Often haunted

‣ Check out Ambrose Bierce's short story "An Occurrence at Owl Creek Bridge" for sophisticated bridge symbolism

‣ Is it a primitive rope bridge? The Golden Gate? Quaint covered wooden? Modern steel?

‣ Often places of danger

‣ What's under the bridge? Troll? Water? Dry creek bed? Deep ravine?

‣ How far down is the drop from the bridge? The farther the fall, the more dangerous.

TWENTY-SIX

SEASONS

There is a season...write, write, write—what? That's not the song's lyrics? Before you write that plot, stop and think about season. Even Southern California has seasons. Sort of.

The symbolism found in seasons has deep roots in literature and life. That's because seasons *really* mattered in ancient times. Agrarian societies depended on seasons to plow, grow, and harvest food. Agriculture united peoples, tribes, and groups. It was a means of achieving wealth. Food is life. So, naturally, seasons, because they are tied to farming and thus food and thus *life*, were fraught with all kinds of symbolic meanings.

Season can:

- Be a plot device.
- Be ironic. Example: a couple finds love

in the dead of winter only to break up in
the summer.
- Be symbolic of a character's personality
  or a character's relationship
- Reveal emotions
- Foreshadow an event, problem, change
  in relationship
- Be thematic
- Be a pattern
- Mirror someone's life

Spring

- The cycle of life's beginning
- Youth and childhood
- Folks are hopeful, fresh, and anticipatory
- New life emerges from plants. Rain
  nourishes new life.
- Buds, flowers, birds, butterflies, and
  sunshine
- Folks sow seeds.
- A fresh start. A new beginning. Rebirth.
  Resurrection.

Summer

- Life is in full swing.
- Young adulthood
- Energy and vitality are abundant

- Romance and passion sizzle during summer's hot months. Example: *Grease*, "summer lovin' happened so fast."
- Food is plentiful. There are vegetables to harvest and fruit hanging from trees.
- In *The Great Gatsby*, on the longest day of the year and in sweltering heat, love, lust, and passion flare up. Thus,
- Increased temperature brings heated arguments and boiling tempers.
- Love and anger are both "hot" emotions.

Fall

- Life is reaped and winding down.
- Middle age
- Folks are fatigued from the harvest or age.
- Harvest is associated with abundance and prosperity.
- Folks give thanks to their god/gods for a plentiful harvest.
- Gratitude for good harvests result in sharing & celebratory feasts.
- A time to count one's blessings.

Winter

- Life is dormant or dead.

- Old age and death
- Often equated with anger, resentment, discontent, or hatred. These emotions are equated with "coldness."
- Worry and anxiety is another emotion associated with this season, because food had to last through the winter. Religious holidays brought joy to the cold dreary days of winter.
- There's a great final scene in the movie version of *Phantom of the Opera*. The old man places a toy on his beloved dead wife's grave. There, in the dismal gray setting and in white snow, lies the Phantom's red rose! A vivid contrast and reminder of passions long ago. The scene would not have been the same had it been any other season.

TWENTY-SEVEN

ANIMALS & CRITTERS

There are many books about symbolic animals, insects, and all that walks, flies, or skitters on the earth. I own several myself. But there are some iconic ones that need little if any explaining because they are so grafted into our history, religion, and mythology.

From feisty felines to kangaroos, animals amuse, captivate, intrigue, and frighten the hell out of us. Animal symbolism is a mixed bag. Example: dogs are symbols for loyalty and friendship, and yet to call someone a dog indicates the person is mean, ugly, or displays animalistic lusts. Macbeth and Julius Caesar equate dogs' temperaments and breeding with men's. Then there's that whole "Let slip the dogs of war" speech by Marc Anthony before all hell breaks loose in Rome after Caesar's assassination.

Demonic Animals

- **Cat/Black cat**: Associated with witchcraft and demons. The black cat was believed a gift from the devil. (They have those creepy demonic-looking eyes too.)
- **Fly:** A symbol of corruption and evil. Bringer of plague and disease. Recall the *Lord of the Flies*? Beelzebub is another name for Satan.
- **Frog**: Associated with magic and the familiar of witches. The frog and its toxic skin is symbolic of evil doings.
- **Grasshopper**: Perhaps derived from Aesop and his ancient tales, the fun-loving grasshopper plays around instead of preparing for the winter (like the ant). When winter arrives, the grasshopper begs for food and shelter from the industrious ant. The ant says, "no way" and the grasshopper dies. The grasshopper is a symbol of human foolishness.
- **He-goats**: A symbol of lust and fertility. With its early links to the Greek gods like Pan (a licentious goat-man), Dionysus (let's get drunk & fornicate god), and Zeus (serial cheater), no

wonder the horns (horny?) and hooves were bestial indicators of the devil.

- **Monkey**: They made an evil comeback as flying goons for the Wicked Witch, but the creature is actually linked to deception and vanity. It's considered one of the three senseless creatures—the other two are tigers (for anger issues) and the deer (for pining love).
- **Snake**: It's a no-brainer. The serpent beguiled Eve into taking a bite of the fruit from the Tree of the Knowledge of Good and Evil.
- **Toad**: A familiar of witches. It's skin may be poisonous.
- **Wolf**: Associated with cruelty, greed, carnality, and dishonesty.

More Animals

- **Bat**: Synonymous with vampires. Bram Stoker's Dracula claimed vampires could control and morph into the creature of the night. The bat's ½ bird, ½ rat appearance makes it the perfect symbol of duplicity. Art depicts demons with bat-like wings.
- **Bear**: Giant, brave, powerful, and fierce.

A symbol of many war gods. Linked to healing, wisdom, and medicine in shamanistic religions.

- **Black Sheep**: A nonconformist, a renegade, does not fit in with the others. In need of direction, spiritual or otherwise.
- **Boar**: Fierce, feral beasts who is quick to attack. The wild boar is symbolic of strength and courage since ancient times.
- **Camel**: Its kneeling posture makes it a symbol of prayer and devotion. The quintessential beast of the desert symbolizes restraint, forbearance, endurance, and humility. It's also a symbol of wealth, the Mercedes of the desert so to speak.
- **Cat:** God or Demon? The cat—small, medium, or lion-sized—has been worshiped for thousands of years. Fierce hunters. Symbol for speed, power, and grace, beauty, and nobility.
- **Cow**: Emblematic of Mother Earth and maternal care. Too bad to call someone a cow means they are fat, stupid, and lazy.
- **Coyote:** Trickster figure in Native American cultures. Symbolic of both common sense and stupidity, its dualism

makes it a creature who transforms and teaches lessons.

- **Dog:** Loyalty, protection, and hunting. Man's best friend.
- **Donkey**: Take your symbolic pick. Either symbolic of indecency and stubbornness *or* humility and endurance.
- **Elephant**: Almost universal symbol for power, strength, wisdom, and steadfastness.
- **Fox**: Sneaky, crafty, sly, treacherous. Another trickster figure.
- **Gazelle**: Grace, goodwill, and swiftness.
- **Goat:** Fertility and lust. Associated with Bacchus (party sex god), Pan, and Zeus. In art, devils and demons are often depicted with hooves and horns. Positive aspects include determination and nimbleness.
- **Hare**: A trickster figure and a symbol of fertility.
- **Hedgehog**: Early Christians deemed the critter evil. Irish witches changed into hedgehogs. Symbol for self-preservation for Native Americans.
- **Hippopotamus:** Symbol of rebirth and renewal to ancient Egyptians.
- **Horse**: Beauty, speed, nobility, and freedom. Associated with the sun and

sky gods. The color of the horse can also be symbolic.

- **Hyena**: Uncleanliness, greed, and cowardice.
- **Jackal**: Evil and destruction in India. Worshiped as the god Anubis in Egypt. Associated with desolation in the bible.
- **Kangaroo**: Speed, and since the kangaroo can go months without water, endurance.
- **Lamb**: Innocence, kindness, and passivity. The Christian symbol for Christ and sacrifice.
- **Mouse**: Meek and lowly.
- **Pig**: On the positive side, it's associated with fertility and abundance. On the negative, gluttony, ignorance, and selfishness.
- **Ox:** Hard work, strength, and prosperity.
- **Raccoon**: Mischievousness. A Native American trickster.
- **Rat**: Good luck in Asian cultures. In the West, it's associated with plague, death, and destruction.
- **Ram**: Virility. Isn't that your first thought when seeing a Dodge ram truck?
- **Rhinoceros**: Vitality, boldness, courage, fertility, and all those alpha-male traits.

- **Stag**: Heralds divine events. Symbolic of hunting and fertility.
- **Wolf**: Romans associated the animal with courage and victory. Now, a symbol of greed, deviousness, and cruelty.

TWENTY-EIGHT

FINAL THOUGHTS

All this information was gathered over the span of many years and using various sources, including books on symbolism and a multitude of online scholarly articles. All explanations are my own, and any duplication of source material is accidental.

What are you going to do with all this new understanding of how iconic symbols can enrich character, conflict, emotions, and themes?

Will your elegantly dressed character trample a pristine red rosebud?

Will they get lost in a foggy forest along a narrow uphill path?

Will they find a clue in the library or the kitchen?

Will they have an argument in a field, a garden, or near a cliff?

Will every door be locked to them?

Will rain drown their sorrows or drench their ambitions or be a plot device?

Will they choke on their food when they realize the truth about something?

Remember, symbolism is never 'this means that.' Symbols and their layered meanings act as a diving board into a deep pool of emotional, psychological, spiritual, cultural, and intellectual dynamics that YOU decide how to mold and manipulate. It's just one more tool for your writing toolbox. A tree can just be a tree. Or not.

Happy writing!

ABOUT THE AUTHOR

Autumn Bardot is a multi-genre author who writes stories about fearless women and dangerous passions. In addition to writing novels, she has taught advanced literary analysis and writing for almost twenty years. Autumn was the featured author on Stoya's Book Club and has an article on writing erotica in BooksbyWomen.org. She was a guest on several podcasts, speaks at writing clubs and reader groups, and leads workshops at writing conferences. Autumn is currently writing her next novel and making videos for new writers on her YouTube channel.

Autumn has a passion for history and a special affinity for the unsung courageous females that history neglects or misunderstands. She lives in Southern California with her husband and ever-growing family. She wishes she was one-tenth as brave as the women she writes about.

Find Autumn on Facebook, Instagram, Twitter, Pinterest, LinkedIn, and YouTube.

OTHER BOOKS BY AUTUMN BARDOT

Autumn's Books
https://amazon.com/author/autumnbardot

Contemporary Fantasy
Goddesses Inc.

Historical Fiction
The Impaler's Wife
Dragon Lady
The Emperor's Assassin

Historical Erotica
Legends of Lust, Erotic Myths from around the
World
Confessions of a Sheba Queen

As LZ Marie
https://amazon.com/author/lzmarie

Urban Fantasy
The Merkabah Recruit

The Merkabah Deception
The merkabah Temptation
The Merkabah Obsession